# Skills Assessments, Grade 1

S0-BSP-868

## Table of Contents

*PLEASE NOTE: Page 34 includes at list of high-frequency words that students should learn to recognize. This list may be given to determine proficiency at the beginning of the year. A copy could be sent home for students to use as homework over an extended period of time.

# Class Record Chart

| Students | Reading Overall Assessment | Match Objects | Group Objects | Letter Recognition | Initial Consonant Sounds | Hear Initial Sounds | Final Consonant Sounds | Medial Consonant Sounds | Initial Blends | Short Vowel Sounds | Long Vowel Sounds | Alliteration | Sound Segmenting | Rhyming Words | High-Frequency Words | Environmental Print | Opposites | Reading Comprehension | Story Sequence | Sentence Structure | Punctuation | Writing Words | Dictation |
|---|---|---|---|---|---|---|---|---|---|---|---|---|---|---|---|---|---|---|---|---|---|---|---|
| | | | | | | | | | | | | | | | | | | | | | | | |
| | | | | | | | | | | | | | | | | | | | | | | | |
| | | | | | | | | | | | | | | | | | | | | | | | |
| | | | | | | | | | | | | | | | | | | | | | | | |
| | | | | | | | | | | | | | | | | | | | | | | | |
| | | | | | | | | | | | | | | | | | | | | | | | |
| | | | | | | | | | | | | | | | | | | | | | | | |
| | | | | | | | | | | | | | | | | | | | | | | | |
| | | | | | | | | | | | | | | | | | | | | | | | |
| | | | | | | | | | | | | | | | | | | | | | | | |
| | | | | | | | | | | | | | | | | | | | | | | | |
| | | | | | | | | | | | | | | | | | | | | | | | |

www.svschoolsupply.com
© Steck-Vaughn Company

Class Record Chart
Skills Assessments 1, SV 7932-4

# Class Record Chart

| Students | Math Overall Assessment | Shapes | Number Recognition | Greater Than, Less Than | Two-Digit Numbers | Counting: 1–10 | Counting: 11–20 | Counting On | Odd or Even | Counting by 10s | Counting by 5s | Counting by 2s | Addition Sentences | Addition | Subtraction Sentences | Subtraction | Word Problems | Ordering Numbers | Numbers to 100 | Ordinal Numbers | Geometric Solids | Patterns | Symmetry | Fractions | Calendar | Time | Estimating Time | Money | Measurement | Reading a Graph |
|---|---|---|---|---|---|---|---|---|---|---|---|---|---|---|---|---|---|---|---|---|---|---|---|---|---|---|---|---|---|---|
| | | | | | | | | | | | | | | | | | | | | | | | | | | | | | | |
| | | | | | | | | | | | | | | | | | | | | | | | | | | | | | | |
| | | | | | | | | | | | | | | | | | | | | | | | | | | | | | | |
| | | | | | | | | | | | | | | | | | | | | | | | | | | | | | | |
| | | | | | | | | | | | | | | | | | | | | | | | | | | | | | | |
| | | | | | | | | | | | | | | | | | | | | | | | | | | | | | | |
| | | | | | | | | | | | | | | | | | | | | | | | | | | | | | | |
| | | | | | | | | | | | | | | | | | | | | | | | | | | | | | | |
| | | | | | | | | | | | | | | | | | | | | | | | | | | | | | | |
| | | | | | | | | | | | | | | | | | | | | | | | | | | | | | | |

Name _____

# Individual Student Chart

| | Test | Retest | | Test | Retest |
|---|---|---|---|---|---|
| **Reading Overall** | | | **Math Overall** | | |
| Match Objects | | | Shapes | | |
| Group Objects | | | Number Recognition | | |
| Letter Recognition | | | Greater Than, Less Than | | |
| Initial Consonant Sounds | | | Two Digit-Numbers | | |
| Hear Initial Sounds | | | Counting: 1–10 | | |
| Final Consonant Sounds | | | Counting: 11–20 | | |
| Medial Consonant Sounds | | | Counting On | | |
| Initial Blends | | | Odd or Even | | |
| Short Vowel Sounds | | | Counting by 10s | | |
| Long Vowel Sounds | | | Counting by 5s | | |
| Alliteration | | | Counting by 2s | | |
| Sound Segmenting | | | Addition Sentences | | |
| Rhyming Words | | | Addition | | |
| High-Frequency Words | | | Subtraction Sentences | | |
| Environmental Print | | | Subtraction | | |
| Opposites | | | Word Problems | | |
| Reading Comprehension | | | Ordering Numbers | | |
| Story Sequence | | | Numbers to 100 | | |
| Sentence Structure | | | Ordinal Numbers | | |
| Punctuation | | | Geometric Solids | | |
| Writing Words | | | Patterns | | |
| Dictation | | | Symmetry | | |
| | | | Fractions | | |
| | | | Calendar | | |
| | | | Time | | |
| | | | Estimating Time | | |
| | | | Money | | |
| | | | Measurement | | |
| | | | Graphs | | |

Name _____  Date _____

# Reading Overall Assessment

**Directions** Darken the circle for the correct answer.

**1.** log

○       ○       ○

**2.**

○     ○     ○     ○

**Directions** Say each picture name.
Circle the letter that stands for the first sound.

**3.**

n   b   m

**4.**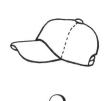

p   t   l

**5.**

s   z   j

**Directions** Say each picture name. Write the beginning vowel sound.

**6.**    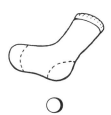      

_____   _____   _____   _____   _____

- - - -   - - - -   - - - -   - - - -   - - - -

_____   _____   _____   _____   _____

Directions: **1.** Have children listen as you read the word. Then, have them darken the circles below the pictures that rhyme. **2.** Have children name the objects. Then, have them darken the circle below the object that does not belong. **3.–6.** Have children listen as you read the directions. Then, have them complete the exercises.

# Reading Overall Assessment, p. 2

**(Directions)** Say each picture name.
Circle the letter that stands for the last sound.

**1.**

s   b   n

**2.**

g   p   f

**3.**

n   s   t

**(Directions)** Darken the circle for the correct answer.

**4.**   sat            stop            sip
          ○              ○              ○

**5.**   said           see            and
          ○              ○              ○

**(Directions)** Say the picture name. Write the word.

**6.**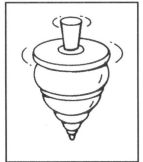

_____

- - - - - - - - - - - - - - - - - - - - - -

_____

Directions: **1.–3.** Read the directions to children and have them complete the exercises. **4.–5.** Say one of the words in each row and have children darken the circle under it. See answer key for words to say. **6.** Read the directions to children and have them complete the exercise.

# Match Objects

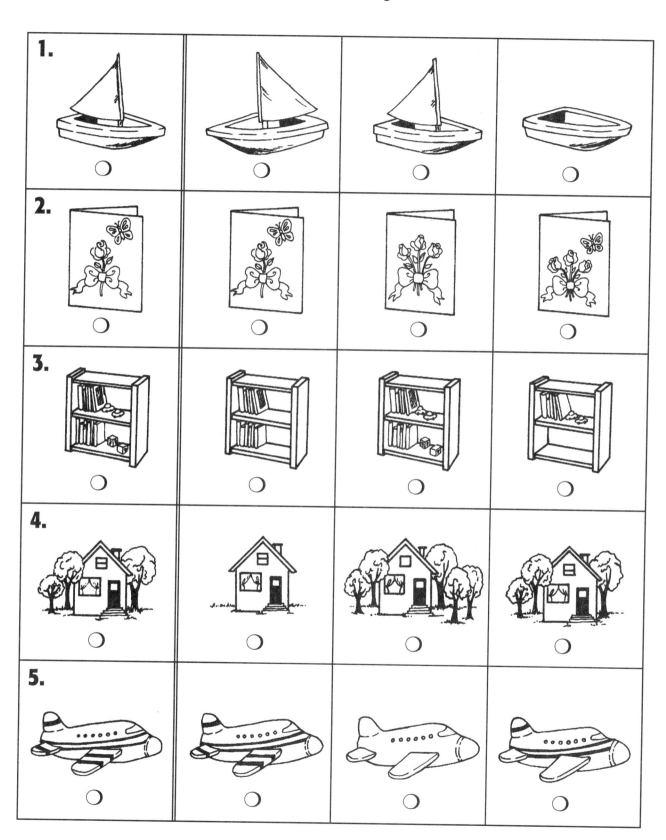

Directions: Have children look at the first picture in each row. Then, have them darken the circle below the one that matches.

# Group Objects

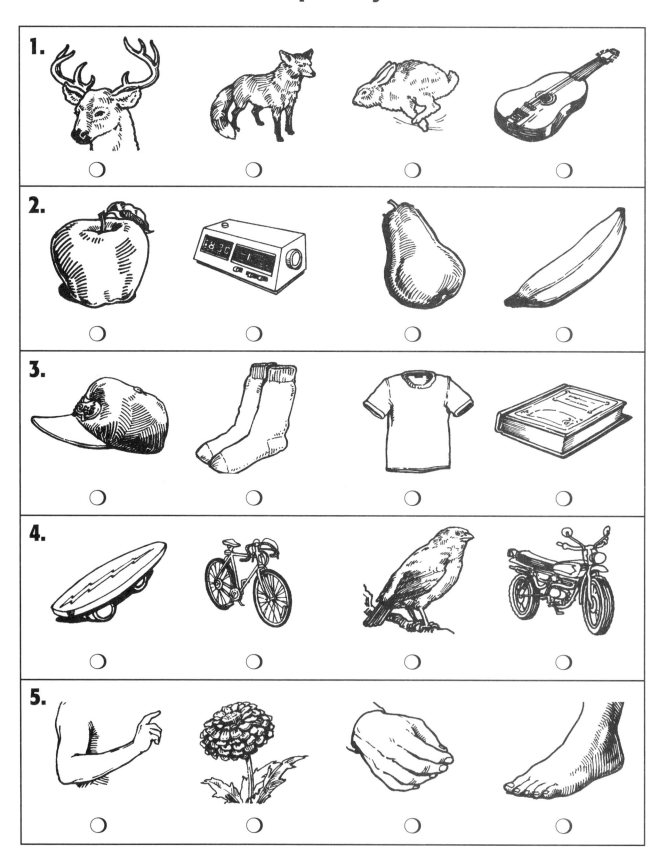

Directions: Have children name the objects in each row. Then, have them darken the circle below the object that does not belong.

# Letter Recognition: Aa, Bb, Cc

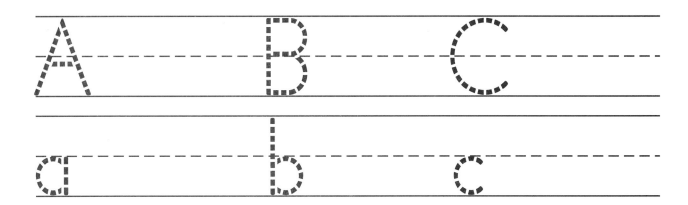

| a | ax        pan        cat |
|---|---------------------------|

| b | baby       job        big |
|---|---------------------------|

| c | cap       face       pack |
|---|---------------------------|

Directions: Have children trace and write the letters on the lines. Then, have them circle the letters that match the letter at the beginning of each row.

Skills Assessments 1, SV 7932-4

Name _____    Date _____

# Letter Recognition: Dd, Ee, Ff

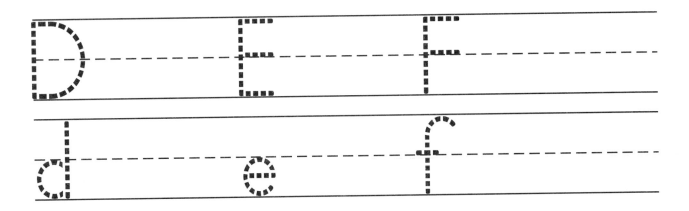

| d | dog | good | dad |
|---|-----|------|-----|

| e | egg | see | red |
|---|-----|-----|-----|

| f | fast | leaf | life |
|---|------|------|------|

Directions: Have children trace and write the letters on the lines. Then, have them circle the letters that match the letter at the beginning of each row.

# Letter Recognition: Gg, Hh, Ii

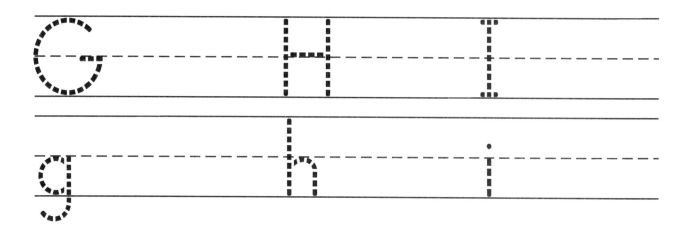

g | gate    soggy    log

h | hill    ashes    arch

i | is    dig    inch

Directions: Have children trace and write the letters on the lines. Then, have them circle the letters that match the letter at the beginning of each row.

# Letter Recognition: Jj, Kk, Ll

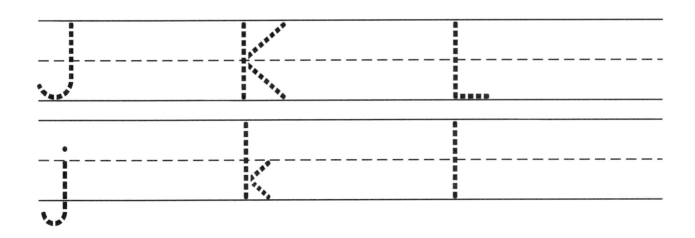

| j | jog | jet | jar |

| k | kick | rake | kite |

| l | lake | hill | milk |

Directions: Have children trace and write the letters on the lines. Then, have them circle the letters that match the letter at the beginning of each row.

# Letter Recognition: Mm, Nn, Oo

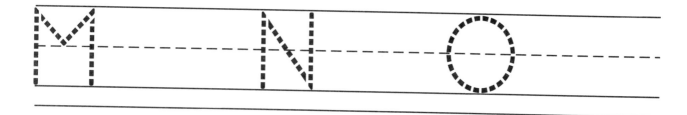

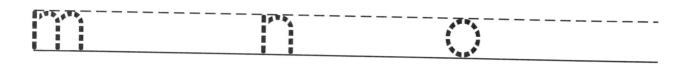

m

| mom | map | ham |
|-----|-----|-----|

n

| not | fun | nine |
|-----|-----|------|

o

| off | hop | too |
|-----|-----|-----|

Directions: Have children trace and write the letters on the lines. Then, have them circle the letters that match the letter at the beginning of each row.

Letter Recognition: Mm, Nn, Oo
Skills Assessments 1, SV 7932-4

# Letter Recognition: Pp, Qq, Rr

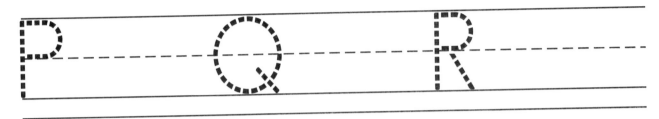

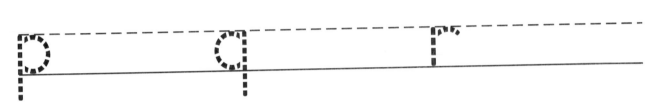

| p | pop | shape | nap |

| q | quack | quit | quilt |

| r | run | purr | where |

Directions: Have children trace and write the letters on the lines. Then, have them circle the letters that match the letter at the beginning of each row.

# Letter Recognition: Ss, Tt, Uu

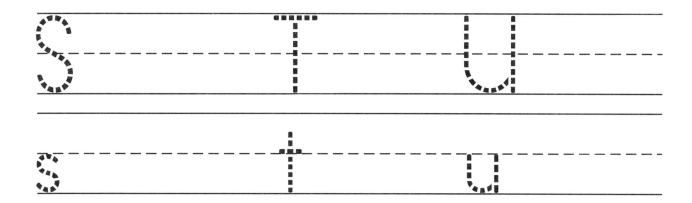

| s | seas | sun | dress |

| t | tent | note | two |

| u | nut | us | pup |

Directions: Have children trace and write the letters on the lines. Then, have them circle the letters that match the letter at the beginning of each row.

# Letter Recognition: Vv, Ww, Xx

V - - - - W - - - - X - - - -

V - - - - W - - - - X - - - -

| v | van | love | vet |

| w | new | was | two |

| x | fox | ax | mix |

**Directions:** Have children trace and write the letters on the lines. Then, have them circle the letters that match the letter at the beginning of each row.

# Letter Recognition: Yy, Zz

Y    Z

y    z

| y | yes | toys | you |
|---|-----|------|-----|

| z | maze | zoo | buzz |
|---|------|-----|------|

Directions: Have children trace and write the letters on the lines. Then, have them circle the letters that match the letter at the beginning of each row.

# Initial Consonant Sounds: b, c, d, f, g

Directions: Have children listen as you say the initial sound for the first picture in each row. Then, have them darken the circles under the pictures in the row that have the same initial sound as the first picture.

# Initial Consonant Sounds: h, j, k, l, m

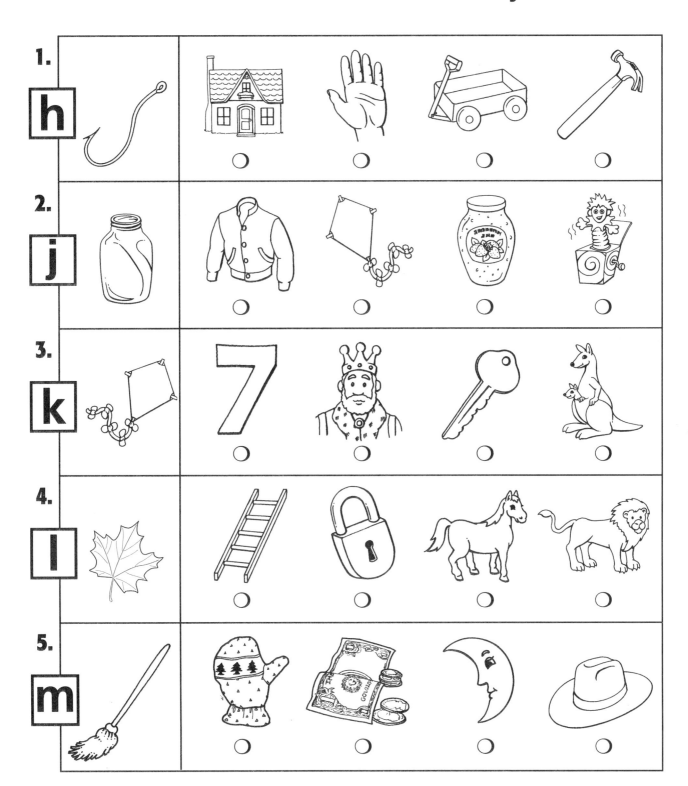

Directions: Have children listen as you say the initial sound for the first picture in each row. Then, have them darken the circles under the pictures in the row that have the same initial sound as the first picture.

# Initial Consonant Sounds: n, p, q, r, s

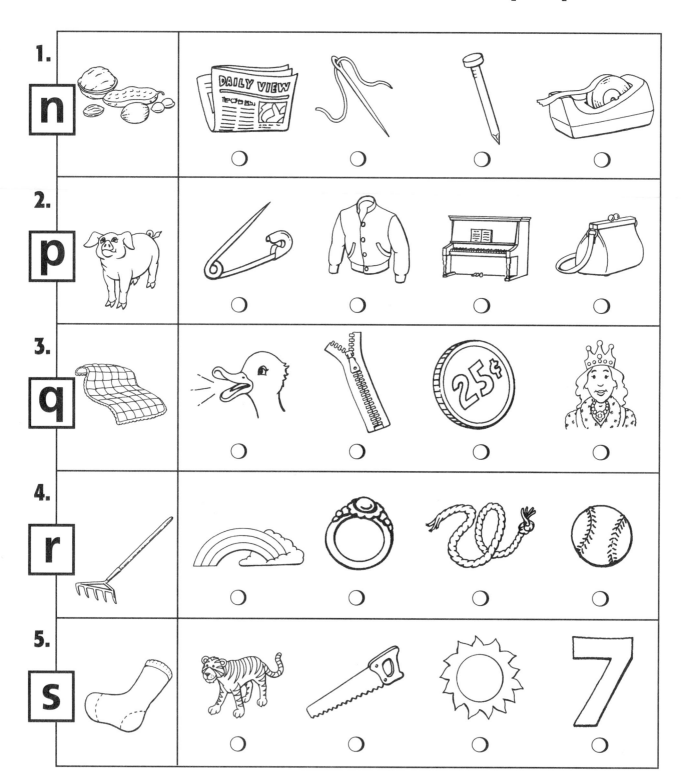

Directions: Have children listen as you say the initial sound for the first picture in each row. Then, have them darken the circles under the pictures in the row that have the same initial sound as the first picture.

# Initial Consonant Sounds: t, v, w, y, z

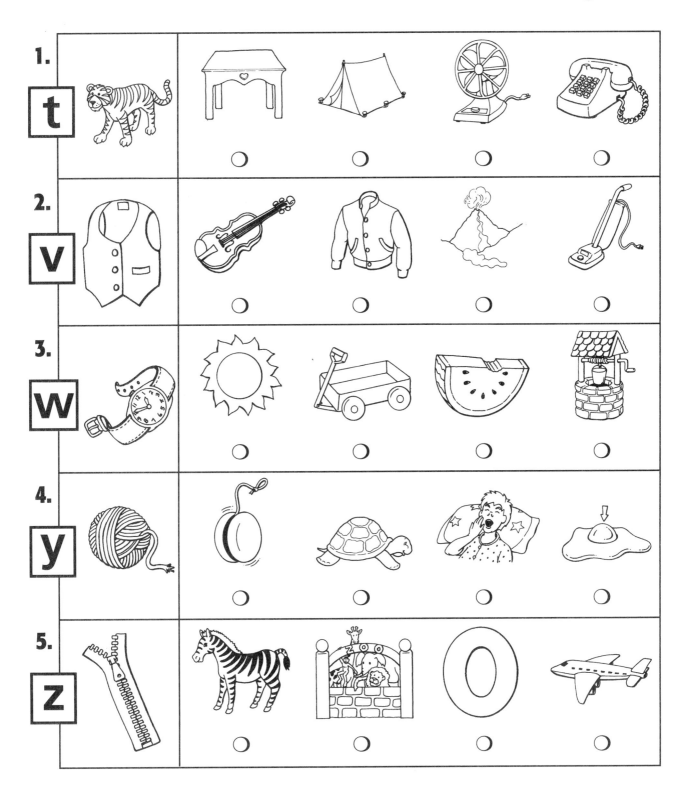

Directions: Have children listen as you say the initial sound for the first picture in each row. Then, have them darken the circles under the pictures in the row that have the same initial sound as the first picture.

# Hear Initial Sounds

**1.**

m   n   r

**2.**

y   w   z

**3.**
10
t   l   d

**4.**

y   w   v

**5.**

g   qu   p

**6.**

d   b   h

**7.**

x   w   y

**8.**

c   g   qu

**9.**

k   h   b

**10.**

s   k   z

**11.**

s   f   t

**12.**

m   h   r

**13.**

n   r   qu

**14.**

w   y   v

**15.**

n   k   h

Directions: Have children listen as you say each picture name. Then, have them circle the letter that stands for the initial sound.

# Final Consonant Sounds: b, d, f, g

**Directions:** Have children listen as you say the final sound for the first picture in each row. Then, have them darken the circles under the pictures in the row that have the same final sound as the first picture.

# Final Consonant Sounds: k, l, m, n

Directions: Have children listen as you say the final sound for the first picture in each row. Then, have them darken the circles under the pictures in the row that have the same final sound as the first picture.

# Final Consonant Sounds: p, r, s, t, v

Directions: Have children listen as you say the final sound for the first picture in each row. Then, have them darken the circles under the pictures in the row that have the same final sound as the first picture.

# Medial Consonant Sounds: b, d, g, k, l

**Directions:** Have children listen as you say the letter sound in each row. Then, have them darken the circles under the pictures in the row that have the same medial sound.

# Medial Consonant Sounds: m, n, p, r, t

**Directions:** Have children listen as you say the letter sound in each row. Then, have them darken the circles under the pictures in the row that have the same medial sound.

# Initial Blends

| | | |
|---|---|---|
| **1.** 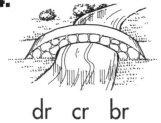<br>sl  st  fr | **2.** <br>gr  tw  cr | **3.** <br>sl  fr  gr |
| **4.** <br>dr  cr  br | **5.** <br>tr  fr  tw | **6.** <br>tr  st  cr |
| **7.** <br>sw  cr  st | **8.** <br>st  sn  br | **9.** <br>dr  fr  sl |
| **10.** <br>st  br  gr | **11.** <br>dr  sl  gr | **12.** <br>st  cr  sk |
| **13.**<br>tw  st  fr | **14.**<br>tr  st  br | **15.**<br>fr  cr  br |

Directions: Have children listen as you say each picture name. Then, have them circle the letters that are the initial blend.

Skills Assessments 1, SV 7932-4

# Short Vowel Sounds

**Directions:** Have children listen as you say the vowel sound for the first picture in each row. Then, have them darken the circles under the pictures in the row that have the same short vowel sound.

Name _____  Date _____

# Long Vowel Sounds

Directions: Have children listen as you say the vowel sound for the first picture in each row. Then, have them darken the circles under the pictures in the row that have the same long vowel sound.

# Alliteration

**1.**

○ same
○ different

**2.**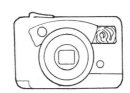

○ same
○ different

**3.**

○ same
○ different

**4.**

○ same
○ different

**5.**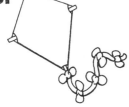

○ same
○ different

**6.**

○ same
○ different

**7.**

○ same
○ different

**8.**

○ same
○ different

Directions: Have children listen as you say the two picture names in each box. Then, have them darken the circle that tells if the two picture names begin with the same sound or two different sounds.

# Sound Segmenting

**1.**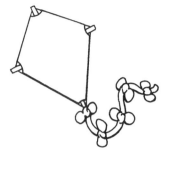
_____

**2.**
_____

**3.**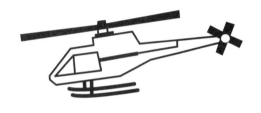
_____

**4.**
_____

**5.**
_____

**6.**
_____

**7.**
_____

**8.**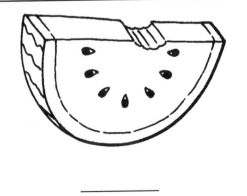
_____

Directions: Have children listen as you emphasize the syllables as you say each picture name. You may wish to have the children say the word with you and clap for each syllable. Then, have them write the number of syllables in each word.

# Rhyming Words

| **1.** sled | | | |
|---|---|---|---|
| | ○ | ○ | ○ |
| **2.** fun | | | |
| | ○ | ○ | ○ |
| **3.** rail | | | |
| | ○ | ○ | ○ |
| **4.** hive | | | |
| | ○ | ○ | ○ |
| **5.** nose | | | |
| | ○ | ○ | ○ |

Directions: Have children listen as you read the word. Then, have them darken the circles below the pictures that rhyme.

# High-Frequency Word List

| | | |
|---|---|---|
| a | here | see |
| am | his | she |
| and | how | that |
| are | I | the |
| can | in | then |
| come | is | they |
| did | it | this |
| do | like | to |
| for | look | what |
| go | me | when |
| good | my | where |
| has | not | who |
| have | now | with |
| he | of | you |
| her | said | your |

Directions: Have children read these high-frequency words. You may wish to have them use the words to write simple rebus sentences.

# Word Recognition: High-Frequency Words

**1.**

see            that            said

○              ○              ○

**2.**

now            you            to

○              ○              ○

**3.**

have           has            she

○              ○              ○

**4.**

look           the            like

○              ○              ○

**5.**

where          what           not

○              ○              ○

Directions: Have children listen as you say the word. Then, have them darken the circle below the word. See answer key for words to say.

# Word Recognition:
# High-Frequency Words, p. 2

**1.**

| with | look | his |
|------|------|-----|
| ○ | ○ | ○ |

**2.**

| my | how | here |
|----|-----|------|
| ○ | ○ | ○ |

**3.**

| am | not | and |
|----|-----|-----|
| ○ | ○ | ○ |

**4.**

| come | can | are |
|------|-----|-----|
| ○ | ○ | ○ |

**5.**

| this | is | they |
|------|-----|------|
| ○ | ○ | ○ |

Directions: Have children listen as you say the word. Then, have them darken the circle below the word. See answer key for words to say.

# Environmental Print

**1.**

STAIR      STOP      SIP

○      ○      ○

**2.**

FOX      ELF      EXIT

○      ○      ○

**3.**

DANGER      DAD      AND

○      ○      ○

**4.**

GET      GO      NOT

○      ○      ○

**5.**

EVEN      TREE      ENTER

○      ○      ○

Directions: Have children listen as you say the word. Then, have them darken the circle below the word. See answer key for words to say.

# Opposites

**1.**

boy

woman ○

girl ○

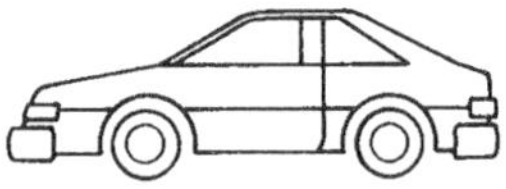

car ○

**2.**

day

seal ○

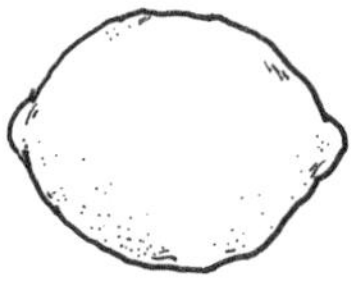

lemon ○

night ○

**3.**

cold

soft ○

hot ○

prickly ○

**4.**

sad

happy ○

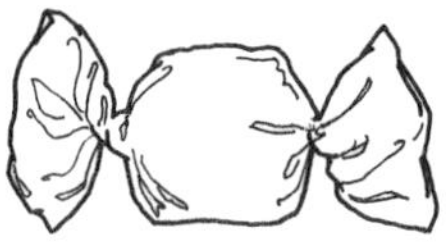

candy ○

yell ○

**5.**

stand

sit ○

dive ○

eat ○

Directions: Have children listen as you say the name of the first picture in each row. Then, have them darken the circle below the picture that is the opposite.

# Reading Comprehension

### A Day at the Zoo

Cindy and her grandfather went to the zoo. They saw elephants, lions, and monkeys. The lions were taking a nap. The monkeys were playing in the trees. Cindy bought peanuts to feed to the elephants. Cindy and her grandfather rode the train around the zoo. They had a fun day.

**1.**

**2.**

**3.**

Directions: Have children listen as you read the story. Then, read each question. Have children darken the circle under the picture that answers the question. **1.** Who took Cindy to the zoo? **2.** Which animal was taking a nap? **3.** What did Cindy feed to the elephants?

# Reading Comprehension, p. 2

## Lucky

Thomas has a new dog. His name is Lucky. He is 3 years old. He likes to play chase with Thomas. He can catch a ball, too. He carries his dish in his mouth when he is hungry. Lucky sleeps on Thomas's bed at night. Thomas loves Lucky.

**1.**

4 years old     3 years old     2 years old

○         ○         ○

**2.**

○         ○         ○

**3.**

○         ○         ○

Directions: Have children listen as you read the story. Then, read each question. Have children darken the circle under the picture that answers the question. **1.** How old is Lucky? **2.** What does Lucky do when he is hungry? **3.** Where does Lucky sleep?

# Story Sequence

**1.**

**2.**

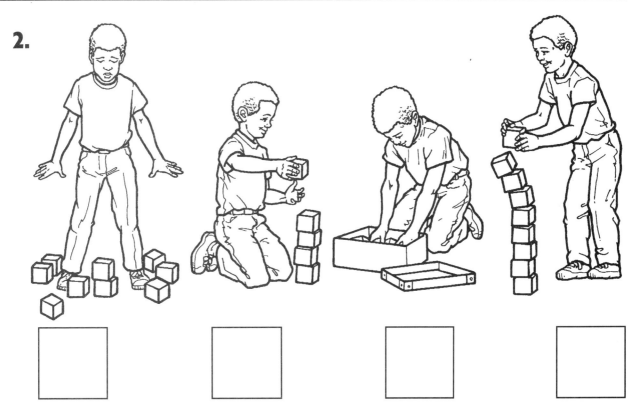

Directions: Have children write the numbers to show the order in which the events happened.

# Sentence Structure

| | |
|---|---|
| **1.** | A cat is in the tree. |

Yes       No

○         ○

| | |
|---|---|
| **2.** | my dog? Where is |

Yes       No

○         ○

| | |
|---|---|
| **3.** | new doll. See my |

Yes       No

○         ○

| | |
|---|---|
| **4.** | Sam said he can play. |

Yes       No

○         ○

| | |
|---|---|
| **5.** | you come? When will |

Yes       No

○         ○

Directions: Have children read the sentences or listen as you read them. Then, have them darken the circle that shows whether or not the correct sentence structure is used.

# Punctuation

| | | |
|---|---|---|
| **1.** | Can you see the dog | |
| | . ○ | ? ○ |

| | | |
|---|---|---|
| **2.** | The car can go fast | |
| | . ○ | ? ○ |

| | | |
|---|---|---|
| **3.** | I am glad you are here | |
| | . ○ | ? ○ |

| | | |
|---|---|---|
| **4.** | Where is my sled | |
| | . ○ | ? ○ |

| | | |
|---|---|---|
| **5.** | Go get the book | |
| | . ○ | ? ○ |

Directions: Have children read the sentences or listen as you read them. Then, have them darken the circle that shows the correct punctuation.

# Writing Words

**1.**

**2.**

**3.**

**4.**

**5.**

Directions: Have children listen as you say the word. Then, have them write the word in the box next to the picture. See answer key for words to say.

# Writing Words, p. 2

| | | |
|---|---|---|
| **1.** | | |
| **2.** | | |
| **3.** | | |
| **4.** | | |
| **5.** | | |

Directions: Have children listen as you say the word. Then, have them write the word in the box next to the picture. See answer key for words to say.

# Dictation

**1.**

_____
- - - - - - - - - - - - - - - - - - - - - - - - - -
_____

**2.**

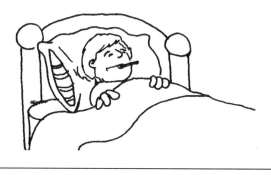

_____
- - - - - - - - - - - - - - - - - - - - - - - - - -
_____

**3.**

_____
- - - - - - - - - - - - - - - - - - - - - - - - - -
_____
- - - - - - - - - - - - - - - - - - - - - - - - - -
_____

Directions: Have children listen as you read the sentence. Then, have them write the sentence on the line below the picture. See answer key for sentences. You may wish to read the sentences twice.

# Dictation, p. 2

**1.**

_____

- - - - - - - - - - - - - - - - - - - - - - - - - -

_____

**2.**

_____

- - - - - - - - - - - - - - - - - - - - - - - - - -

_____

**3.**

_____

- - - - - - - - - - - - - - - - - - - - - - - - - -

_____

Directions: Have children listen as you read the sentence. Then, have them write the sentence on the line below the picture. See answer key for sentences. You may wish to read the sentences twice.

Name _____     Date _____

# Math Overall Assessment

**(Directions)** Darken the circle for the correct answer.

**1.**     7, 5, 8      ○      5, 6, 7      ○      8, 9, 5      ○

**2.**

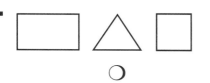      ○      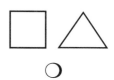      ○      ○

**(Directions)** Color the correct bead.

**3.**

**(Directions)** Count and write the number.

**4.**

_____

**5.**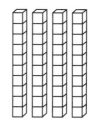

_____

**(Directions)** Solve and write the answer.

**6.**    2      7
     + 3    + 2
     ___     ___

**7.**    4      5
     − 2    − 1
     ___     ___

Directions: **1.** Have children darken the circle under the numbers that are in the correct order. **2.** Have children darken the circle under the picture that shows a square and a triangle only. **3.** Have children darken the seventh bead. **4.–5.** Have children write the number that tells how many. **6.–7.** Have children write the answers.

# Math Overall Assessment, p. 2

**Directions** Draw what comes next.

1. ☐  △  ◯  ☐  △  ◯  ☐  _____

**Directions** Darken the circle for the correct answer.

2.           △

  ◯                    ◯                    ◯

3.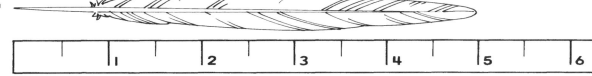

  6 inches          5 inches          7 inches

  ◯                    ◯                    ◯

4.           5.

  12¢          3¢                    4¢          8¢

  ◯            ◯                    ◯            ◯

6.      (clock showing ~4:00)     (clock showing ~7:00)     (clock showing ~10:00)

  ◯                    ◯                    ◯

Directions: **1.** Have children draw what comes next in the pattern. **2.** Have them darken the circle under the one that shows one half. **3.** Have children look at the object. Then, have them darken the circle under the correct length. **4.–5.** Have children look at the coins and darken the circle under the correct value. **6.** Have children darken the circle under the clock that shows 7:00.

# Shapes

**1.**

**2.**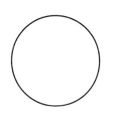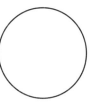

**3.**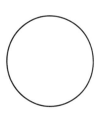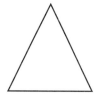

**4.**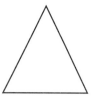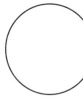

**5.**

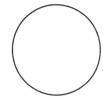   

Directions: Have children circle the shape that matches the shape in the first box of each row.

# Number Recognition: 1, 2, 3

1

2

3

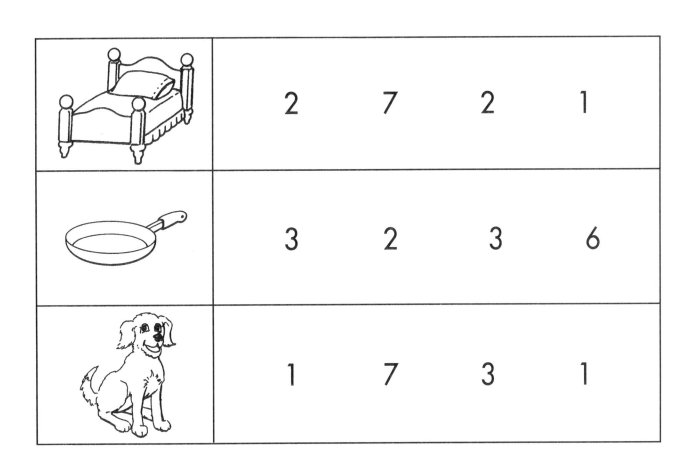

| | | | | |
|---|---|---|---|---|
| | 2 | 7 | 2 | 1 |
| | 3 | 2 | 3 | 6 |
| | 1 | 7 | 3 | 1 |

**Directions:** Have children trace and write the numbers on the lines. Then, have them point to the picture at the beginning of each row and circle the number that you say. See answer key for numbers to say.

# Number Recognition: 4, 5, 6

4 - - - - - - - - - - - - - - - -

5 - - - - - - - - - - - - - - - -

6 - - - - - - - - - - - - - - - -

| | | | | |
|---|---|---|---|---|
| (cup) | 7 | 4 | 5 | 4 |
| (broom) | 8 | 6 | 6 | 3 |
| (hat) | 5 | 4 | 5 | 3 |

**Directions:** Have children trace and write the numbers on the lines. Then, have them point to the picture at the beginning of each row and circle the number that you say. See answer key for numbers to say.

# Number Recognition: 7, 8, 9

7

8

9

| | | | | |
|---|---|---|---|---|
|  ★ | 9 | 7 | 9 | 5 |
| 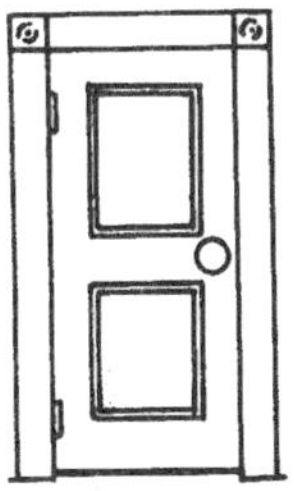 🚪 | 3 | 9 | 8 | 8 |
|  ☀ | 7 | 5 | 7 | 6 |

Directions: Have children trace and write the numbers on the lines. Then, have them point to the picture at the beginning of each row and circle the number that you say. See answer key for numbers to say.

# Number Recognition: 0, 10

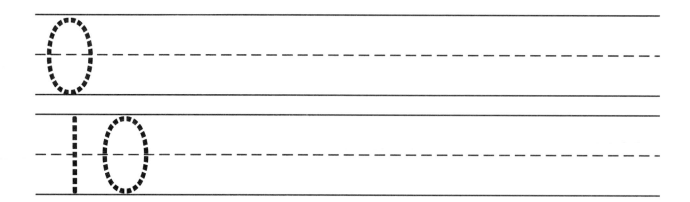

| | | | | |
|---|---|---|---|---|
|  | 9 | 8 | 9 | 0 |
| | 10 | 7 | 10 | 1 |

Directions: Have children trace and write the numbers on the lines. Then, have them point to the picture at the beginning of each row and circle the number that you say. See answer key for numbers to say.

# Greater Than, Less Than

**1.**

9 7

○ ○

**2.**

7 5

○ ○

**3.**

4 6

○ ○

**4.**

8 10

○ ○

**5.**

5 3

○ ○

**6.**

6 8

○ ○

**7.**

6 4

○ ○

**8.**

2 4

○ ○

**9.**

8 3

○ ○

**10.**

9 5

○ ○

Directions: Have children listen as you say the number. Then, have them darken the circle that tells the number that is greater or less than. **1.** Which number is greater than 8? **2.** greater than 6? **3.** less than 5? **4.** greater than 9? **5.** less than 4? **6.** less than 7? **7.** greater than 5? **8.** less than 3? **9.** less than 6? **10.** greater than 7?

# Two-Digit Numbers

**1.**

33          23          42
○           ○           ○

**2.**

75          62          52
○           ○           ○

**3.**

76          51          37
○           ○           ○

**4.**

42          23          34
○           ○           ○

**5.**

45          41          50
○           ○           ○

Directions: Have children listen as you say the number. See the answer key for numbers. Then, have children darken the circle below the number that you say.

# Counting: 1–10

**1.**

9      8      6

**2.**

4      3      6

**3.**

2      4      5

**4.**

8      10      9

**5.**

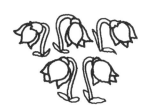

3      2      5

**6.**

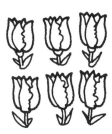

7      6      5

**7.**

7      9      10

**8.**

9      7      6

Directions: Have children count the objects in the box. Then, have them circle the number that tells how many.

# Counting: 11–15

| 1. | 11   12 |
|----|---------|
|    | 14   10 |

| 2. | 16   15 |
|----|---------|
|    | 14   13 |

| 3. | 10   12 |
|----|---------|
|    | 13   11 |

| 4. | 13   15 |
|----|---------|
|    | 12   11 |

| 5. | 15   16 |
|----|---------|
|    | 14   13 |

Directions: Have children count the objects. Then, have them circle the number that tells how many.

# Counting: 16–20

| 1. | 17 | 15 |
| --- | --- | --- |
| | 18 | 16 |

| 2. | 18 | 19 |
| --- | --- | --- |
| | 20 | 17 |

| 3. | 15 | 16 |
| --- | --- | --- |
| | 18 | 17 |

| 4. | 18 | 19 |
| --- | --- | --- |
| | 17 | 20 |

| 5. | 16 | 17 |
| --- | --- | --- |
| | 18 | 19 |

Directions: Have children count the objects. Then, have them circle the number that tells how many.

Name _____     Date _____

# Counting On

**1.** | 3

**2.** | 5

**3.** | 6

**4.** | 8

**5.** | 7

Directions: Have children look at the number on the bag. Then, have them darken the circle below the picture that shows how many more pieces of fruit are needed to equal the number you say. **1.** Count on to have 6 apples in the bag. **2.** Count on to have 9 pears. **3.** Count on to have 12 oranges. **4.** Count on to have 12 bananas. **5.** Count on to have 10 cherries.

Name _____     Date _____

# Odd or Even

**1.**

even                    odd

**2.**

even                    odd

**3.**

even                    odd

**4.**

even                    odd

**5.**

even                    odd

**6.**

even                    odd

**7.**

even                    odd

**8.**

even                    odd

Directions: Have children circle pairs of dots. Then, have them circle the answer that tells if the number of dots is even or odd.

# Counting by 10s

**1.**

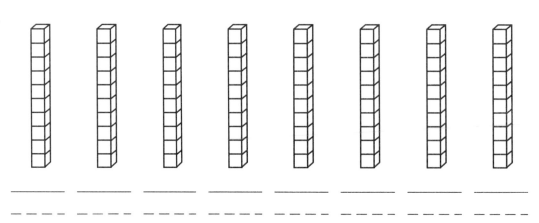

_____

\- \- \- \- \- \- \- \- \- \- \- \- \- \- \- \-

_____

**2.**

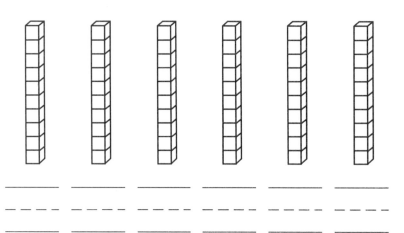 

_____

\- \- \- \- \- \- \- \- \- \- \- \-

_____

**3.**

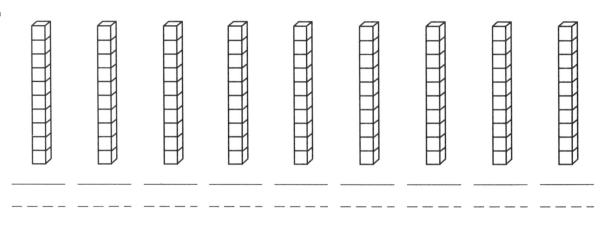

_____

\- \- \- \- \- \- \- \- \- \- \- \- \- \- \- \- \- \-

_____

Directions: Have children skip count by 10s. Then, have them write the number for each set of 10 to tell how many.

# Counting by 5s

5          10          15          _____

25          _____          _____          40

_____          50          55          _____

_____          _____          75          _____

85          _____          _____          100

Directions: Have children skip count by 5s. Then, have them write the missing numbers that complete the pattern.

# Counting by 2s

2     4     ___     8     ___

12     ___     16     18     ___

___     ___     26     ___     30

Directions: Have children skip count by 2s. Then, have them write the missing numbers that complete the pattern.

# Addition Sentences

**1.**

___ + ___ = ___

**2.**

___ + ___ = ___

**3.**

___ + ___ = ___

**4.**

___ + ___ = ___

**5.**

___ + ___ = ___

**6.**

___ + ___ = ___

**7.**

___ + ___ = ___

**8.**

___ + ___ = ___

Directions: Have children write addition sentences and solve.

# Addition: Sums to 5

1.  2
   + 2
   ____

2.  3
   + 2
   ____

3.  1
   + 1
   ____

4.  3
   + 0
   ____

5.  1
   + 3
   ____

6.  4
   + 1
   ____

7.  3
   + 1
   ____

8.  2
   + 0
   ____

9.  0
   + 5
   ____

10.  2
    + 1
    ____

11.  1
    + 4
    ____

12.  0
    + 4
    ____

13.  1
    + 2
    ____

14.  2
    + 3
    ____

15.  0
    + 3
    ____

16.  5
    + 0
    ____

Directions: Have children write the sums.

# Addition: Sums to 6, 7, and 8

**1.**  1
   + 5
   _____

**2.**  4
   + 2
   _____

**3.**  5
   + 2
   _____

**4.**  6
   + 2
   _____

**5.**  2
   + 5
   _____

**6.**  3
   + 3
   _____

**7.**  6
   + 1
   _____

**8.**  0
   + 7
   _____

**9.**  4
   + 4
   _____

**10.**  3
   + 5
   _____

**11.**  6
   + 0
   _____

**12.**  5
   + 3
   _____

**13.**  1
   + 7
   _____

**14.**  4
   + 3
   _____

**15.**  8
   + 0
   _____

**16.**  3
   + 4
   _____

Directions: Have children write the sums.

# Addition: Sums to 9 and 10

1.   9
   + 1
   ___

2.   0
   + 10
   ___

3.   1
   + 8
   ___

4.   5
   + 5
   ___

5.   7
   + 3
   ___

6.   5
   + 4
   ___

7.   8
   + 2
   ___

8.   9
   + 0
   ___

9.   3
   + 6
   ___

10.   7
    + 2
    ___

11.   3
    + 7
    ___

12.   4
    + 5
    ___

13.   2
    + 8
    ___

14.   6
    + 4
    ___

15.   8
    + 1
    ___

16.   6
    + 3
    ___

Directions: Have children write the sums.

# Subtraction Sentences

**1.**

$$4 - 2 = \underline{\hspace{1cm}}$$

**2.**

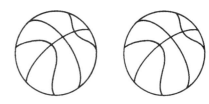

$$2 - 1 = \underline{\hspace{1cm}}$$

**3.**

$$5 - 2 = \underline{\hspace{1cm}}$$

**4.**

$$6 - 2 = \underline{\hspace{1cm}}$$

**5.**

$$3 - 3 = \underline{\hspace{1cm}}$$

**6.**

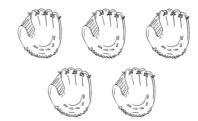

$$5 - 1 = \underline{\hspace{1cm}}$$

**7.**

$$6 - 3 = \underline{\hspace{1cm}}$$

**8.**

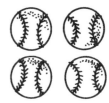

$$4 - 3 = \underline{\hspace{1cm}}$$

Directions: Have children write an X on the objects to find the answer.

**Subtraction Sentences**
Skills Assessments 1, SV 7932-4

# Subtraction from 5 and Less

1.      3
      − 0
    ──────

2.      5
      − 1
    ──────

3.      4
      − 2
    ──────

4.      2
      − 1
    ──────

5.      2
      − 0
    ──────

6.      5
      − 4
    ──────

7.      5
      − 5
    ──────

8.      3
      − 2
    ──────

9.      4
      − 0
    ──────

10.      5
       − 2
     ──────

11.      4
       − 1
     ──────

12.      5
       − 3
     ──────

13.      4
       − 3
     ──────

14.      3
       − 1
     ──────

15.      5
       − 0
     ──────

16.      4
       − 4
     ──────

Directions: Have children write the answers.

# Subtraction from 6, 7, and 8

1.    7
    − 4
    _____

2.    6
    − 1
    _____

3.    8
    − 6
    _____

4.    7
    − 6
    _____

5.    8
    − 3
    _____

6.    7
    − 2
    _____

7.    6
    − 3
    _____

8.    8
    − 8
    _____

9.    8
    − 1
    _____

10.    7
    − 5
    _____

11.    6
    − 5
    _____

12.    8
    − 4
    _____

13.    6
    − 2
    _____

14.    7
    − 4
    _____

15.    8
    − 7
    _____

16.    7
    − 0
    _____

Directions: Have children write the answers.

Name _____  Date _____

# Subtraction from 9 and 10

**1.**  10
       − 5
       _____

**2.**  9
       − 6
       _____

**3.**  10
       − 7
       _____

**4.**  9
       − 0
       _____

**5.**  10
       − 10
       _____

**6.**  9
       − 3
       _____

**7.**  10
       − 2
       _____

**8.**  10
       − 9
       _____

**9.**  9
       − 4
       _____

**10.**  10
        − 8
        _____

**11.**  9
        − 7
        _____

**12.**  9
        − 1
        _____

**13.**  10
        − 4
        _____

**14.**  9
        − 9
        _____

**15.**  9
        − 5
        _____

**16.**  10
        − 1
        _____

Directions: Have children write the answers.

# Word Problems

| | |
|---|---|
| **1.** Andy ate 3 cookies. Lisa ate 2 cookies. How many cookies did Andy and Lisa eat altogether? | 3<br><br>5<br><br>2 |
| **2.** If you have 3 red balls, 3 blue balls, and 1 green ball, how many balls do you have in all? | 7<br><br>3<br><br>6 |
| **3.** Juan picked 4 red roses. Maria picked 4 yellow roses. How many roses did they have in all? | 7<br><br>9<br><br>8 |
| **4.** Tina's cat had 5 spotted kittens, 1 black kitten, and 1 white kitten. How many kittens did she have in all? | 5<br><br>7<br><br>6 |

Directions: Have children listen as you read the word problems. Then, have them circle the number that tells how many.

# Word Problems, p. 2

**1.** The Jackson family takes a hike.

Mrs. Jackson sees 4 🌿 .

Then she sees 2 more.

How many 🌿 in all?

_____ ◯ _____ = _____ 🌿

**2.** Mr. Jackson finds 3 🌰 .

Then he finds 4 more.

How many 🌰 in all?

_____ ◯ _____ = _____ 🌰

**3.** Mike watches 5 🐿️.

Then 4 run away.

How many 🐿️ are left?

_____ ◯ _____ = _____ 🐿️

**4.** Ellen sees 7 🐸 .

Then 3 hop away.

How many 🐸 are left?

_____ ◯ _____ = _____ 🐸

Directions: Have children listen as you read the word problems. Then, have them write the number sentences and solve.

# Ordering Numbers

**1.**

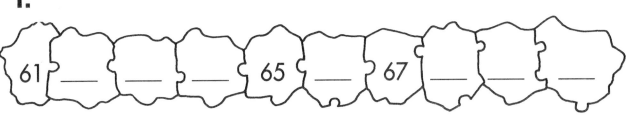

61 ___ ___ ___ 65 ___ 67 ___ ___ ___

**2.**

56 57 ___ ___ ___ 61 ___ ___ ___ ___

**3.**

___ ___ 23 24 ___ ___ ___ ___ ___ 30

**4.**

45 46 ___ ___ ___ 50 ___ ___ ___ 54

**5.**

89 ___ ___ 92 ___ ___ 95 ___ 97 ___

Directions: Have children write the missing numbers.

**www.svschoolsupply.com**
© Steck-Vaughn Company

**Ordering Numbers**
Skills Assessments 1, SV 7932-4

# Numbers to 100

| 1 | | | | | | | | | 10 |
|---|---|---|---|---|---|---|---|---|---|
| | | | | | | | | | 20 |
| | | | | | | | | | 30 |
| | | | | | | | | | 40 |
| | | | | | | | | | 50 |
| | | | | | | | | | 60 |
| | | | | | | | | | 70 |
| | | | | | | | | | 80 |
| | | | | | | | | | 90 |
| | | | | | | | | | 100 |

Directions: Have children write the missing numbers to fill in the grid.

# Ordinal Numbers

**1.**

**2.**

**3.**

**4.**

**5.**

**6.**

Directions: Have children color the bird in each row that shows the order. **1.** first; **2.** fourth; **3.** sixth; **4.** third; **5.** second; **6.** fifth

# Geometric Solids

**1.**

**2.**

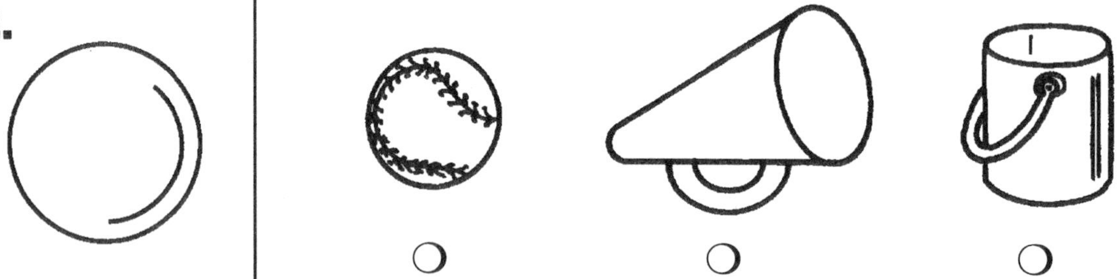

**3.**

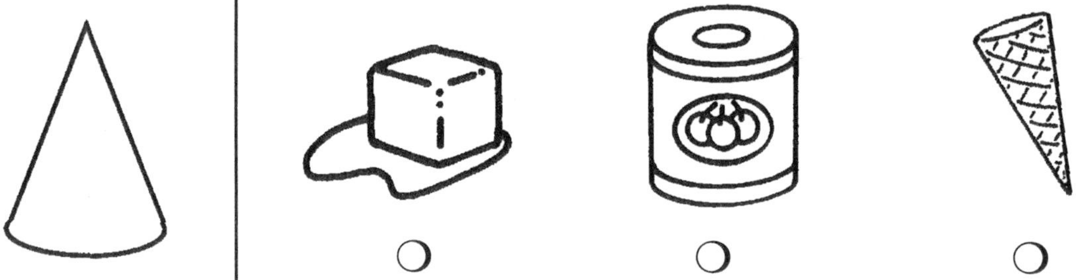

**4.**

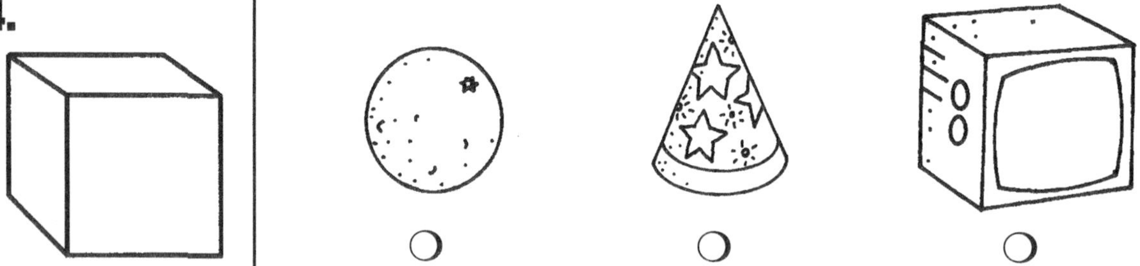

**5.**

Directions: Have children look at the picture in the first box. Then, have them darken the circle below the picture that has the same shape.

# Patterns: Shape

**1.**

**2.**

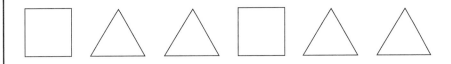

**3.**

**4.**

**5.**

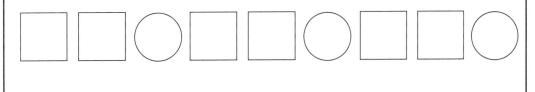

Directions: Have children look at the pattern. Then, have them draw the shape that comes next in the pattern.

# Patterns: Size

**1.**

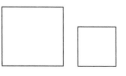    

**2.**

**3.**

**4.**

**5.**

Directions: Have children look at the pattern. Then, have them draw the one that comes next in the pattern.

# Patterns: Number

**1.**

1   2   1   2   1   2   1   ___ ___ ___

**2.**

1   2   3   1   2   3   1   ___ ___ ___

**3.**

2   4   6   2   4   6   ___ ___ ___ ___

**4.**

3   3   5   3   3   5   ___ ___ ___ ___

**5.**

5   6   7   8   5   6   7   ___ ___ ___

Directions: Have children write the numbers that come next in the pattern.

# Symmetry

**1.**

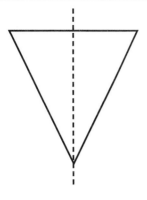

yes    no

**2.**

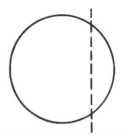

yes    no

**3.**

yes    no

**4.**

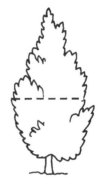

yes    no

**5.**

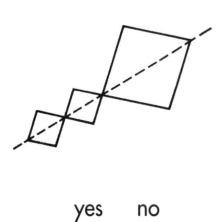

yes    no

**6.**

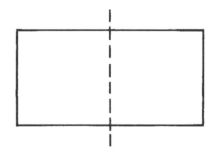

yes    no

Directions: Have children look at each shape. Then, have them circle the answer to tell if the two parts match.

# Fractions

**1.**

**2.**

**3.**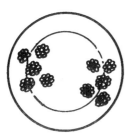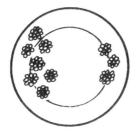

**4.**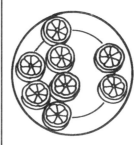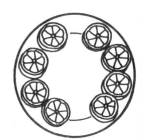

**5.**

**6.**

Directions: Have children circle the pictures that show equal shares.

# Fractions, p. 2

**1.**

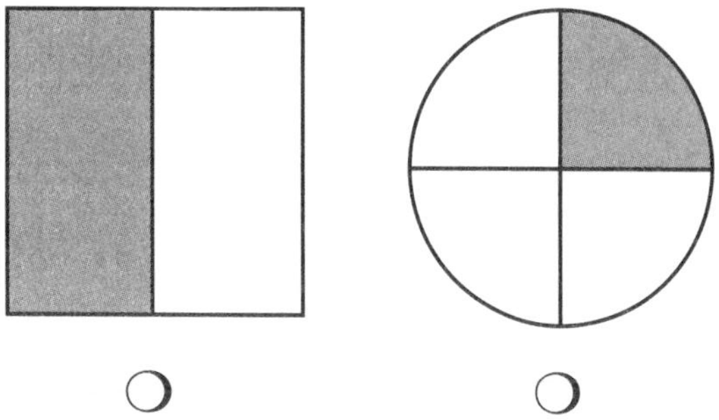

**2.**

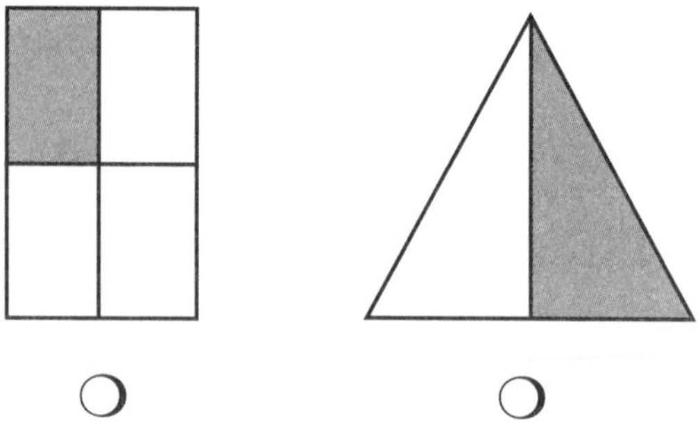

**3.**

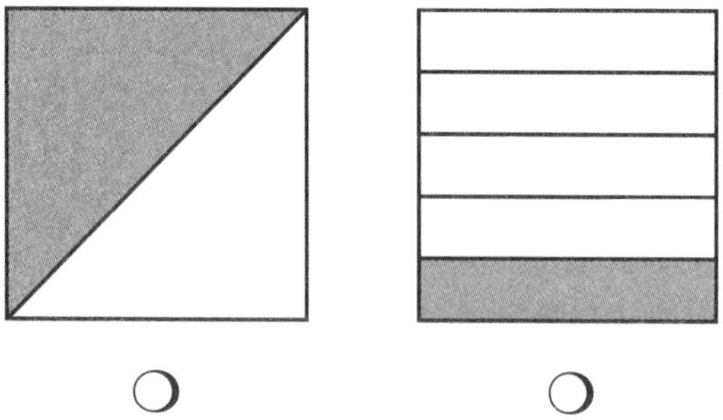

**4.**

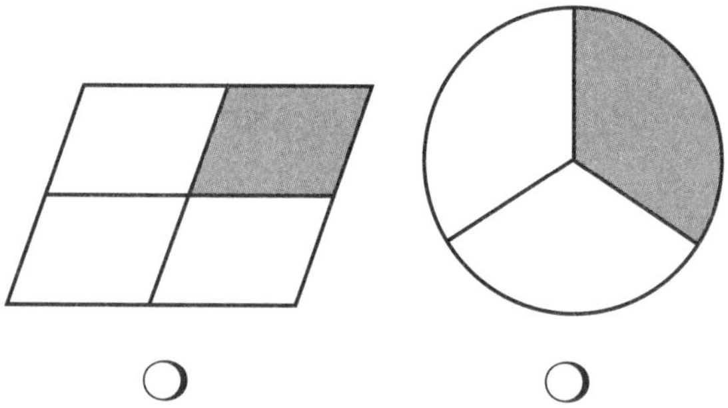

**5.**

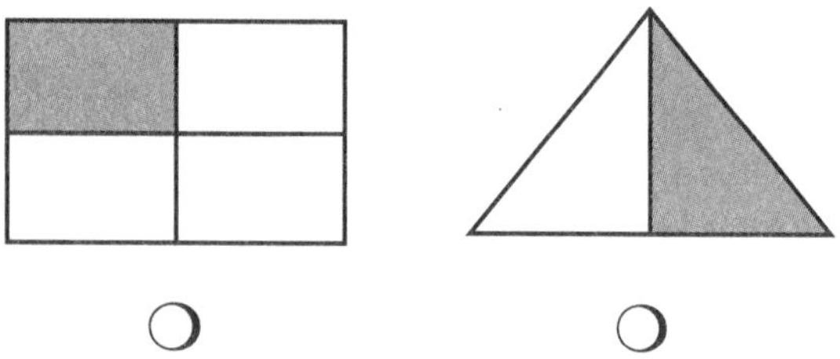

**6.**

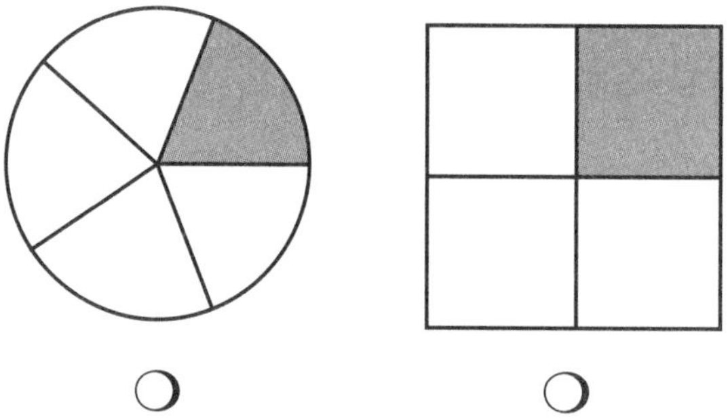

**7.**

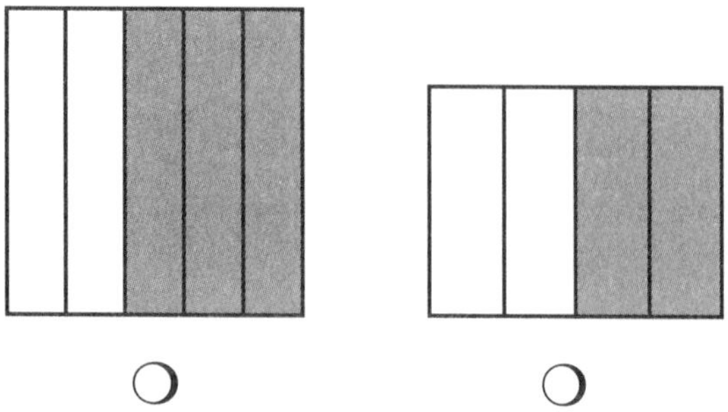

**8.**

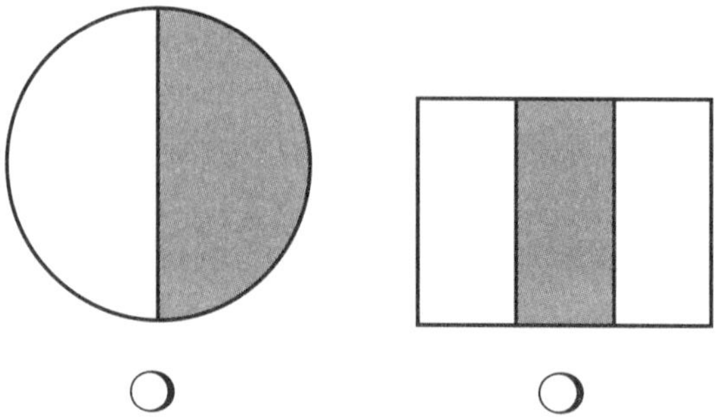

Directions: Have children listen as you say each fraction. Then, have them darken the circle below the one that shows the fraction.
**1.** one half; **2.** one fourth; **3.** one half; **4.** one fourth; **5.** one fourth; **6.** one fourth; **7.** one half; **8.** one half.

# Calendar

| Sunday | Monday | Tuesday | Wednesday | Thursday | Friday | Saturday |
|--------|--------|---------|-----------|----------|--------|----------|
|  |  | 1 | 2 | 3 | 4 | 5 |
| 6 | 7 | 8 | 9 | 10 | 11 | 12 |
| 13 | 14 | 15 | 16 | 17 | 18 | 19 |
| 20 | 21 | 22 | 23 | 24 | 25 | 26 |
| 27 | 28 | 29 | 30 |  |  |  |

**1.**

3rd

Tuesday ○  Thursday ○  Friday ○

**2.**

16th

Monday ○  Tuesday ○  Wednesday ○

**3.**

20th

Sunday ○  Saturday ○  Monday ○

Directions: Have children listen as you say the date in the first box. Then, have them darken the circle that tells the day of the week.

# Time: Analog

**1.**

○        ○        ○

**2.**

○        ○        ○

**3.**

○        ○        ○

**4.**

○        ○        ○

Directions: Have children listen as you say the time. Then, have them darken the circle below the clock that shows the time.
See answer key for times to say.

# Time: Digital

**1.**

**2.**

**3.**

**4.**

**5.**

**6.**

**7.**

**8.**

**9.**

Directions: Have children read the time on the clock. Then, have them write the time in the box below.

# Estimating Time

**1.**

**2.**

**3.**

**4.**

Directions: Have children look at each pair of pictures. Then, have them circle the one that takes more time to complete.

# Money: Identifying Coins

| 1. | | | |
|----|---|---|---|
| nickel | ○ | ○ | ○ |
| 2. | | | |
| penny | ○ | ○ | ○ |
| 3. | | | |
| quarter | ○ | ○ | ○ |
| 4. | | | |
| nickel | ○ | ○ | ○ |
| 5. | | | |
| dime | ○ | ○ | ○ |

Directions: Have children listen as you say the coin name. Then, have them darken the circle under the correct coin.

# Money: Identifying Values

| | | | |
|---|---|---|---|
| **1.**  | 1¢ ○ | 5¢ ○ | 15¢ ○ |
| **2.**  | 5¢ ○ | 1¢ ○ | 10¢ ○ |
| **3.**  | 10¢ ○ | 11¢ ○ | 1¢ ○ |
| **4.**  | $5.00 ○ | $1.00 ○ | $10.00 ○ |
| **5.**  | 25¢ ○ | 5¢ ○ | 15¢ ○ |

Directions: Have children look at the picture in the first box. Then, have them darken the circle under the money value.

Name _____     Date _____

# Money: Counting

**1.**

5¢      4¢      3¢

**2.**

7¢      6¢      5¢

**3.**

10¢      8¢      5¢

**4.**

15¢      5¢      25¢

**5.**

5¢      10¢      2¢

**6.**

5¢      1¢      10¢

**7.**

6¢      5¢      7¢

**8.**

16¢      6¢      3¢

Directions: Have children look at the picture of the coins. Then, have them circle the money value.

**Money: Counting**
Skills Assessments 1, SV 7932-4

# Measurement: Centimeters

**1.**

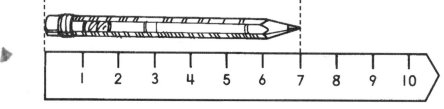

| 8 cm | 7 cm | 6 cm |
|:---:|:---:|:---:|
| ○ | ○ | ○ |

**2.**

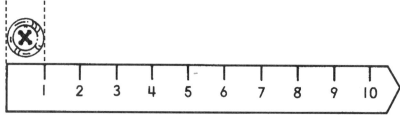

| 2 cm | 3 cm | 1 cm |
|:---:|:---:|:---:|
| ○ | ○ | ○ |

**3.**

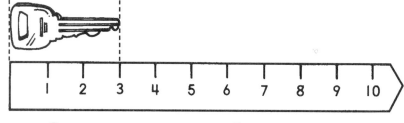

| 2 cm | 3 cm | 4 cm |
|:---:|:---:|:---:|
| ○ | ○ | ○ |

**4.**

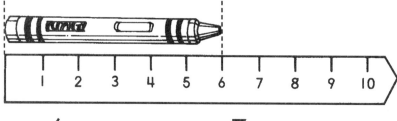

| 6 cm | 7 cm | 5 cm |
|:---:|:---:|:---:|
| ○ | ○ | ○ |

Directions: Have children look at the object. Then, have them darken the circle under the correct length.

# Measurement: Inches

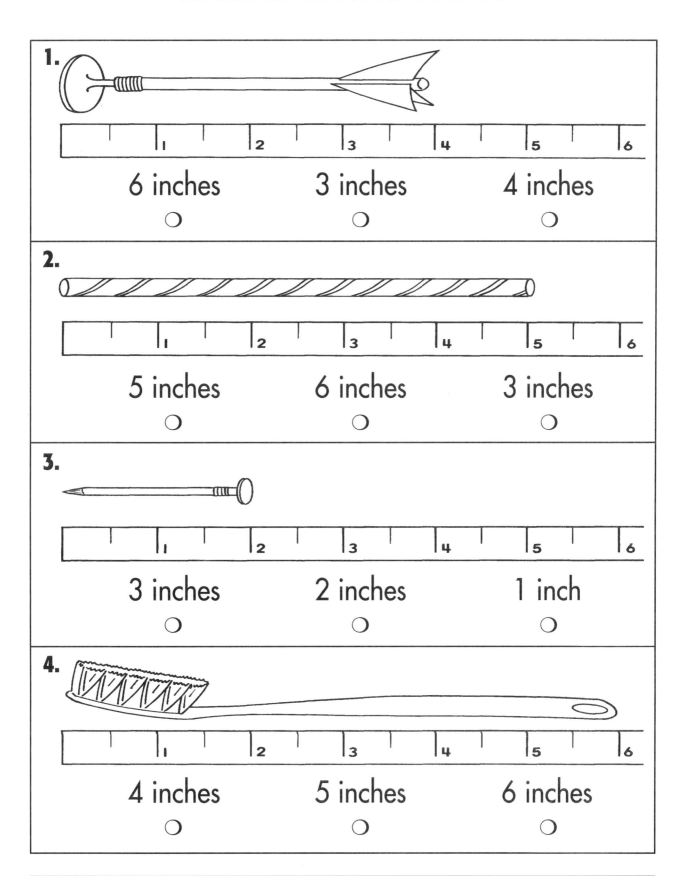

**1.**

6 inches          3 inches          4 inches
○                 ○                 ○

**2.**

5 inches          6 inches          3 inches
○                 ○                 ○

**3.**

3 inches          2 inches          1 inch
○                 ○                 ○

**4.**

4 inches          5 inches          6 inches
○                 ○                 ○

Directions: Have children look at the object. Then, have them darken the circle under the correct length.

# Reading a Graph

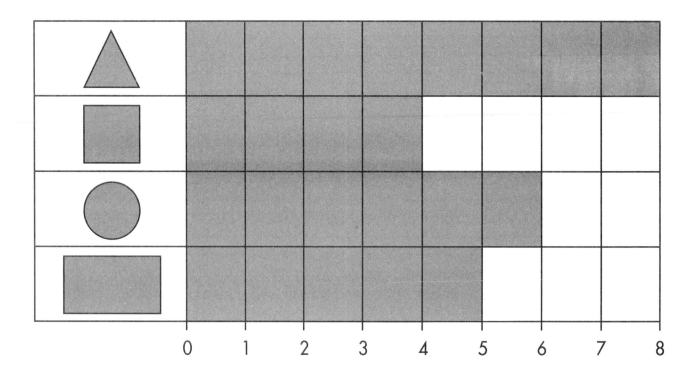

| | 1. | | |
|---|---|---|---|
| 1. | 6 ○ | 8 ○ | 7 ○ |
| 2. | 7 ○ | 5 ○ | 8 ○ |
| 3. | 5 ○ | 6 ○ | 4 ○ |
| 4. | 5 ○ | 4 ○ | 3 ○ |

Directions: Have children listen as you say the shape. Then, have them read the graph and darken the circle that tells how many.
1. circle; 2. triangle; 3. rectangle; 4. square.

# Skills Assessments, Grade 1
## Answer Key

**Page 5**
1. frog, dog
2. Banana is not something to wear.
3. m
4. t
5. s
6. a, e, u, i, o

**Page 6**
1. s
2. p
3. t
4. stop
5. and
6. Check students' work for correct spelling of *top*.

**Page 7**
1. third boat
2. second card
3. third bookshelf
4. fourth house
5. second plane

**Page 8**
1. guitar
2. radio
3. book
4. bird
5. flower

**Page 9**
Check students' work.

**Page 10**
Check students' work.

**Page 11**
Check students' work.

**Page 12**
Check students' work.

**Page 13**
Check students' work.

**Page 14**
Check students' work.

**Page 15**
Check students' work.

**Page 16**
Check students' work.

**Page 17**
Check students' work.

**Page 18**
1. bird, bat, basket
2. comb, camera, carrot
3. deer, dog, desk
4. football, five, fork
5. girl, guitar, gate

**Page 19**
1. house, hand, hammer
2. jacket, jam, jack-in-the-box
3. king, key, kangaroo
4. ladder, lock, lion
5. mitten, money, moon

**Page 20**
1. newspaper, needle, nail
2. pin, piano, purse
3. quack, quarter, queen
4. rainbow, ring, rope
5. saw, sun, seven

**Page 21**
1. table, tent, telephone
2. violin, volcano, vacuum
3. wagon, watermelon, well
4. yoyo, yawn, yolk
5. zebra, zoo, zero

**Page 22**
1. m 2. z 3. t
4. w 5. qu 6. d
7. y 8. g 9. k
10. s 11. f 12. r
13. n 14. v 15. h

**Page 23**
1. tub, cub, bib
2. hand, dad, rod
3. roof, half, leaf
4. bag, leg, bug

**Page 24**
1. chalk, fork, milk
2. camel, seal, squirrel
3. ham, gum, jam
4. ten, queen, man

**Page 25**
1. ship, mop, map
2. bear, car, door
3. skates, plus, gas
4. ant, hat, cot
5. glove, wave, dive

**Page 26**
1. robot, robin
2. ladder, medal
3. wagon, tiger
4. monkey, jacket, joker
5. ruler, violin

**Page 27**
1. lemon, woman
2. rainbow, pencil
3. paper, puppet
4. squirrel, turtle, bird
5. guitar, letter

**Page 28**
1. sl 2. gr 3. fr
4. br 5. tw 6. cr
7. sw 8. sn 9. dr
10. br 11. dr 12. cr
13. st 14. tr 15. fr

**Page 29**
1. pen, vest, ten
2. mask, lamp, van
3. drum, duck, rug
4. sock, blocks, frog
5. bib, pig, king

**Page 30**
1. queen, seal
2. jay, sail, game
3. tube, fuse
4. goat, hoe, robe
5. bike, pie, sky

**Page 31**
1. same
2. different
3. same
4. same
5. different
6. same
7. different
8. same

**Page 32**
1. 1 2. 2 3. 4 4. 2
5. 3 6. 3 7. 2 8. 4

**Page 33**
1. bread, bed
2. run, sun
3. sail, tail
4. five, dive
5. rose, hose

**Page 35**
1. see
2. you
3. have
4. like
5. what

**Page 36**
1. with
2. here
3. and
4. come
5. this

**Page 37**
1. STOP
2. EXIT
3. DANGER
4. GO
5. ENTER

**Page 38**
1. girl
2. night
3. hot
4. happy
5. sit

**Page 39**
1. grandfather
2. lion
3. peanuts

**Page 40**
1. 3 years old
2. holds his dish in his mouth
3. sleeps on the bed

**Page 41**
1. 3 4 1 2
2. 4 2 1 3

**Page 42**
1. yes
2. no
3. no
4. yes
5. no

**Page 43**
1. ?
2. .
3. .
4. ?
5. .

**Page 44**
1. sun
2. pig
3. map
4. cot
5. desk

**Page 45**
1. net
2. lid
3. cap
4. tub
5. sled

**Page 46**
1. See the big dog.
2. Sam is ill.
3. The girls like to pla(y).

**Page 47**
1. The cat is soft.
2. Jim likes to fish.
3. The jet can go fast.

**Page 48**
1. 5, 6, 7
2. square and triangle only
3. Color the 7th bead.
4. 12
5. 40
6. 5, 9
7. 2, 4

**Page 49**
1. triangle
2. one half triangle
3. 5 inches
4. 12¢
5. 8¢
6. 7:00

**Page 50**
1. large square
2. large circle
3. large rectangle
4. large triangle
5. large rectangle

**Page 51**
bed: 2
pan: 3
dog: 1

**Page 52**
cup: 4
mop: 6
hat: 5

**Page 53**
star: 9
door: 8
sun: 7

**Page 54**
bird: 9
turtle: 10

**Page 55**
1. 9 2. 7 3. 4 4. 10
5. 3 6. 6 7. 6 8. 2 9. 3
10. 9

**Page 56**
1. 23
2. 52
3. 76
4. 34
5. 41

**Page 57**
1. 8 2. 4 3. 5 4. 9
5. 3 6. 6 7. 10 8. 7

**Page 58**
1. 12
2. 14
3. 11
4. 13
5. 15

**Page 59**
1. 17
2. 19
3. 16
4. 20
5. 18

**Page 60**
1. 3 apples
2. 4 pears
3. 6 oranges
4. 4 bananas
5. 3 cherries

**Page 61**
1. even  2. odd
3. even  4. even
5. odd  6. even
7. odd  8. odd

**Page 62**
1. 10, 20, 30, 40, 50, 60, 70, 80
2. 10, 20, 30, 40, 50, 60
3. 10, 20, 30, 40, 50, 60, 70, 80, 90

**Page 63**
20; 30; 35; 45; 60; 65; 70; 80; 90; 95

**Page 64**
6; 10; 14; 20; 22; 24; 28

**Page 65**
1. 2 + 1 = 3
2. 2 + 3 = 5
3. 3 + 2 = 5
4. 5 + 1 = 6
5. 2 + 2 = 4
6. 2 + 4 = 6
7. 4 + 1 = 5
8. 3 + 1 = 4

**Page 66**
1. 4 2. 5 3. 2 4. 3
5. 4 6. 5 7. 4 8. 2
9. 5 10. 3 11. 5 12. 4
13. 3 14. 5 15. 3 16. 5

**Page 67**
1. 6 2. 6 3. 7 4. 8
5. 7 6. 6 7. 7 8. 7
9. 8 10. 8 11. 6 12. 8
13. 8 14. 7 15. 8 16. 7

**Page 68**
1. 10 2. 10 3. 9 4. 10
5. 10 6. 9 7. 10 8. 9
9. 9 10. 9 11. 10 12. 9
13. 10 14. 10 15. 9 16. 9

**Page 69**
1. 2 2. 1 3. 3 4. 4
5. 0 6. 4 7. 3 8. 1

**Page 70**
1. 3 2. 4 3. 2 4. 1
5. 2 6. 1 7. 0 8. 1
9. 4 10. 3 11. 3 12. 2
13. 1 14. 2 15. 5 16. 0

**Page 71**
1. 3 2. 5 3. 2 4. 1
5. 5 6. 5 7. 3 8. 0
9. 7 10. 2 11. 1 12. 4
13. 4 14. 3 15. 1 16. 7

**Page 72**
1. 5 2. 3 3. 3 4. 9
5. 0 6. 6 7. 8 8. 1
9. 5 10. 2 11. 2 12. 8
13. 6 14. 0 15. 4 16. 9

**Page 73**
1. 5
2. 7
3. 8
4. 7

**Page 74**
1. 4 + 2 = 6
2. 3 + 4 = 7
3. 5 − 4 = 1
4. 7 − 3 = 4

**Page 75**
1. 62, 63, 64, 66, 68, 69, 70
2. 58, 59, 60, 62, 63, 64, 65
3. 21, 22, 25, 26, 27, 28, 29
4. 47, 48, 49, 51, 52, 53
5. 90, 91, 93, 94, 96, 98

**Page 76**
Check students' work.

**Page 77**
1. first
2. fourth
3. sixth
4. third
5. second
6. fifth

**Page 78**
1. tissue box
2. baseball
3. ice cream cone
4. television
5. vegetable can

**Page 79**
1. circle
2. square
3. circle
4. triangle
5. square

**Page 80**
1. large square
2. large circle
3. small triangle
4. small circle
5. medium square

**Page 81**
1. 2 1 2
2. 2 3 1
3. 2 4 6 2
4. 3 3 5 3
5. 8 5 6

**Page 82**
1. yes
2. no
3. yes
4. no
5. yes
6. yes

**Page 83**
1.–6. Check students' work.

**Page 84**
1. one half of square
2. one fourth of rectangle
3. one half of square
4. one fourth of parallelogram
5. one fourth of rectangle
6. one fourth of square
7. one half of rectangle
8. one half of circle

**Page 85**
1. Thursday
2. Wednesday
3. Sunday

**Page 86**
1. 5:00
2. 9:00
3. 2:00
4. 6:00

**Page 87**
1. 1:00
2. 4:00
3. 7:00
4. 3:00
5. 6:00
6. 9:00
7. 11:00
8. 2:00
9. 10:00

**Page 88**
1. big book
2. lots of dishes
3. paint the wall
4. 100 piece puzzle

**Page 89**
1. nickel
2. penny
3. quarter
4. nickel
5. dime

**Page 90**
1. 5¢
2. 10¢
3. 1¢
4. $1.00
5. 25¢

**Page 91**
1. 3¢ 2. 6¢ 3. 10¢ 4. 25¢
5. 10¢ 6. 5¢ 7. 5¢ 8. 16¢

**Page 92**
1. 7 cm
2. 1 cm
3. 3 cm
4. 6 cm

**Page 93**
1. 4 inches
2. 5 inches
3. 2 inches
4. 6 inches

**Page 94**
1. 6
2. 8
3. 5
4. 4